POCKET ★★★★ MICHELLE OBAMA WISDOM ★★★★

UNOFFICIAL

**WISE AND INSPIRATIONAL WORDS
FROM MICHELLE OBAMA**

POCKET ★★★★
MICHELLE
OBAMA
WISDOM ★ ★ ★ ★

UNOFFICIAL

WISE AND INSPIRATIONAL WORDS
FROM MICHELLE OBAMA

Hardie Grant

BOOKS

CONTENTS

MICHELLE OBAMA ON...

WOMEN

'I decided that I wasn't bossy. I was strong. I wasn't loud. I was a young woman with something important to say.'

Black Girls Rock Awards, 28th March 2015

'There is no limit to what we,
as women, can accomplish.'

Campaiqn video, 'First Lady Michelle Obama
answers your Twitter questions', 31st May 2012

'As women, we must
stand up for each other.'

Speech at the State Department Women
of Courage Awards, 11th March 2009

'I was surrounded by
extraordinary women
in my life who taught
me about quiet strength
and dignity.'

TED Talk, 'First Lady Michelle Obama:
A passionate, personal case for education',
2nd April 2009

'I am always irritated by
the "You can have it all"
statement. It's a ridiculous
aspiration. I don't want
women out there to have the
expectation that if they're
not having it all, then
somehow they're failing.'

In conversation with Oprah Winfrey at the
United State of Women Summit, 14th June 2016

'I told [young women] that
they should disregard
anyone who demeans or
devalues them, and that
they should make their
voices heard in the world.'

Speech at Hillary for America campaign event,
13th October 2016

WOMEN

'We need to do a better job
at putting ourselves higher
on our own "to-do" list.'

Marie Claire, 16th January 2015

WOMEN

'I am so proud to be
a woman today and
every single day.'

Speech at the State Department Women
of Courage Awards, 11th March 2009

MICHELLE OBAMA ON...

FAMILY

'I think it's important for
both parents to shoulder
that [responsibility].'

Parade, 15th August 2013

'We as parents are
their most important
role models.'

Speech at Democratic National Convention,
25th July 2016

FAMILY

'The security of your
parents' love really
gives you the foundation
to think that you can fly.
And then you do.'

Essence, May 2009

FAMILY

'My most important title
is still "mum-in-chief".
My daughters are still
the heart of my heart and
the centre of my world.'

Speech at Democratic National Convention,
4th September 2012

'My mother's love has
always been a sustaining
force for our family, and
one of my greatest joys
is seeing her integrity,
her compassion, her
intelligence reflected
in my daughters.'

One Nation Speech, Democratic National
Convention, 25th August 2008

FAMILY

'My father's life is a testament to that basic American promise that no matter who you are or how you started out, if you work hard you can build a decent life for yourself and an even better life for your kids.'

Speech at Barack Obama campaign event, 13th August 2012

'Happiness for me
is when my kids are
good and when my
family is whole.'

Prevention, 3rd November 2011

'Reach for partners that make you better. Do not bring people in your life who weigh you down.'

In conversation with Elizabeth Garrett Anderson students, 25th May 2011

MICHELLE OBAMA ON...

HERSELF

'The most important thing
to me is raising strong
women and raising my
daughters well... I think
that is the most important
job that I will ever have.'

In conversation with Elizabeth Garrett Anderson
students, 25th May 2011

HERSELF

'It would be hard
for me to edit myself
and still be me.'

Marie Claire, 22nd October 2008

'I never cut class. I loved getting As, I liked being smart. I liked being on time. I thought being smart is cooler than anything in the world.'

Telegraph, 2nd April 2009

'I am an example of what
is possible when girls
from the very beginning
are loved and nurtured
by people around them.'

In conversation with Elizabeth Garrett Anderson
students, 25th May 2011

'When I hear about
negative and false attacks,
I really don't invest any
energy in them, because
I know who I am.'

Marie Claire, 22nd October 2008

'It takes a lot of patience
to be the President
of the United States.
I'm not that patient.'

The View, 24th September 2012

'One of the lessons that
I grew up with was to
always stay true to
yourself and never let
what somebody else
says distract you from
your goals.'

Marie Claire, 22nd October 2008

★★★

HERSELF

'I want to be this really
fly 80-, 90 year-old.'

Parade, 15th August 2013

HERSELF

'I was not raised with
wealth or resources
or any social standing
to speak of.'

In conversation with Elizabeth Garrett Anderson
students, 25th May 2011

'I have never felt more
confident in myself,
more clear on who
I am as a woman.'

Parade, 15th August 2013

MICHELLE OBAMA ON...

BARACK

BARACK

'[Barack is] always asking: "Is that new? I haven't seen that before." It's like, Why don't you mind your own business? Solve world hunger. Get out of my closet.'

The New York Times, 20th March 2009

BARACK

'There are so many ways to
serve and being President
is one of the hardest
ways and that's one of the
reasons why I tell Barack,
I'm a little smarter than him.
I picked the easier job.'

The View, 25th May 2012

BARACK

'I think my husband is cute
so you know, more power
to the people who think
he's cute as well!'

Chicago Tribune, 21st July 2007

BARACK

[When asked if Barack picks up his socks]

'No, no, no he doesn't...
He thinks he's neat, but he
has people who help him...
and I'm like, it's not you
who's neat, the people who
pick up your socks, those
are the neat people.'

The Ellen Show, 2nd February 2012

'We try to do date nights;
it's a little tough. Barack has
a 20-car motorcade, men
with guns, the ambulance
is always there. How
romantic can you be?'

Late Night with Jimmy Fallon, 23rd February 2013

'Today, I love my husband even more than I did four years ago... even more than I did 23 years ago, when we first met. I love that he's never forgotten how he started.'

Speech at the Democratic National Convention, 4th September 2012

'I love that we can trust
Barack to do what he says
he's going to do, even
when it's hard – especially
when it's hard.'

Speech at the Democratic National Convention,
5th September 2012

'Barack and I were raised with so many of the same values: like you work hard for what you want in life, that your word is your bond and you do what you say you're going to do.'

One Nation Speech, Democratic National Convention, 25th August 2008

MICHELLE OBAMA ON...

SUCCESS

'I want you to understand
that every scar that you
have is a reminder not
just that you got hurt,
but that you survived.'

Martin Luther King Junior Preparatory School
Commencement Address, 9th June 2015

'Success doesn't count,
unless you earn it fair
and square.'

Speech at the Democratic National Convention,
4th September 2012

'I learned to turn stumbles and missteps into sources of motivation. A week with three tests and two papers wasn't a reason to stress out, but a reason to plan.'

Eastern Kentucky University Commencement Address, 11th May 2013

SUCCESS

'How hard you work
matters much more than
how much you make.'

Speech at the Democratic National Convention,
4th September 2012

'Whether you come from
a council estate or a country
estate, your success will
be determined by your own
confidence and fortitude.'

Telegraph, 2nd April 2012

'Instead of letting your hardships and failures discourage or exhaust you, let them inspire you Let them make you even hungrier to succeed.'

Martin Luther King Junior Preparatory School
Commencement Address, 9th June 2015

SUCCESS

'Success is only
meaningful and
enjoyable if it feels
like your own.'

Daily Mail, 18th June 2012

★★

SUCCESS

'When times get tough and
fear sets in, think of those
people who paved the way
for you and those who are
counting on you to pave
the way for them.'

University of California-Merced Commencement
Address, 16th May 2009

'There will be all kinds
of folks who are eager to
help you, but they are not
going to come knocking
on your door to find you.'

Martin Luther King Junior Preparatory School
Commencement Address, 9th June 2015

SUCCESS

'Success isn't about how much money you make, it's about the difference you make in people's lives.'

Speech at the Democratic National Convention, 4th September 2012

★★

SUCCESS

'Be the best that
you can be.'

Telegraph, 2nd April 2012

SUCCESS

'Instead of letting those
feelings defeat you,
let them motivate you.'

Martin Luther King Junior Preparatory School
Commencement Address, 9th June 2015

MICHELLE OBAMA ON...
LIFE

'You're not supposed
to do this perfectly.
You don't do life perfectly.
No one does.'

Seventeen, May 2016

'We're in this together.'

Speech on International Women's Day
at Let Girls Learn Event, 8th March 2016

'A full life means giving
  back to our community
  and our country.'

'Sign up to serve' video, 12th January 2013

'Good relationships feel
good. They feel right.
They don't hurt.'

In conversation with Elizabeth Garrett Anderson
students, 25th May 2011

'With every word you speak, with every choice you make, with the way you carry yourself each day, you are rewriting the story of our communities.'

Martin Luther King Junior Preparatory School Commencement Address, 9th June 2015

'When you've worked hard, and done well, and walked through the doorway of opportunity, you do not slam it shut behind you. No, you reach back.'

Speech at the Democratic National Convention, 5th September 2012

'As painful as they are,
those holes we all have
in our hearts are what truly
connect us to each other.'

Martin Luther King Junior Preparatory School
Commencement Address, 9th June 2015

LIFE

'Who's in your life, and
do you respect them,
and do they respect you?'

In conversation with Elizabeth Garrett Anderson
students, 25th May 2011

'We should always have three
friends in our lives – one who
walks ahead whom we look
up to and follow; one who
walks beside us, who is with
us every step of our journey;
and then, one whom we reach
back for and bring along
after we've cleared the way.'

Speech at the National Mentoring Summit,
25th January 2011

'There are still so many causes worth sacrificing for. There is still so much history yet to be made.'

Keynote Address at Young African Women
Leaders Forum, 22nd June 2011

MICHELLE OBAMA ON...

EDUCATION

'Neither of my parents
and hardly anyone in the
neighbourhood where
I grew up went to college...
I had the opportunity to
attend some of the finest
universities in this country.
... For me, education
was power.'

CNN, 13th October 2016

'That's the one thing people can't take away from you... your education.'

Speech at the National Arts and Humanities Youth Program Awards, 15th November 2016

'There is no boy, at this age, cute enough or interesting enough to stop you from getting an education... If I had worried about who liked me and who thought I was cute when I was your age, I wouldn't be married to the President of the United States.'

Glamour magazine's 'The Power of an Educated Girl panel', 29th September 2015

'My education was truly
the starting point for every
opportunity I've had in
my life.'

Speech at 'Let Girls Learn' event, 18th March 2016

'No country can ever
truly flourish if it stifles
the potential of its women
and deprives itself of
the contributions of half
of its citizens.'

Speech at the Summit of the Mandela Washington
Fellowship for Young African Leaders,
30th July 2014

'It's also about attitudes
and beliefs – the belief that
girls simply aren't worthy
of an education, that women
should have no role outside
the home.'

Speech at 'Let Girls Learn' event, 18th March 2016

'My education has been the key to everything.'

Marie Claire, 19th December 2016

'Don't just be book-smart,
be smart about the world
– know your community,
know your politics.'

Speech at Mulberry School for Girls,
16th June 2015

MICHELLE OBAMA ON...

COURAGE

COURAGE

'People who are truly strong lift others up. People who are truly powerful bring others together.'

Speech at Hillary for America Campaign Event,
13th October 2016

COURAGE

'Real change comes from having enough comfort to be really honest and say something very uncomfortable.'

The New York Times, 18th June 2008

COURAGE

'When someone is cruel
or acts like a bully, you
don't stoop to their level.
No, our motto is, when
they go low, we go high.'

Speech at Democratic National Convention,
25th July 2016

COURAGE

'I plan to keep speaking
out on the behalf [of young
people], not just for the rest
of my time as First Lady,
but for the rest of my life.'

Marie Claire, 19th December 2016

'When I think about the
country I want to give my
children, it's not the world
we have now. All I have
to do is look into the faces
of my children, and I realise
how much work we need
to do.'

Vanity Fair, December 2007

★★★

COURAGE

'There is nothing that
any of you can't do.'

Speech at the National Arts and Humanities
Youth Program Awards, 15th November 2016

'While our circumstances
may be different, in so
many ways, the solutions to
our struggles are the same.'

Speech at International Woman of Courage
Awards, 4th March 2014

COURAGE

'I am desperate for change
– now – not in eight years
or 12 years, but right now.'

Vanity Fair, 27th December 2007

COURAGE

'No matter who you are,
no matter where you come
from, you are beautiful.'

Speech at Black Girls Rock Awards,
28th March 2015

'Don't ever underestimate the importance you can have, because history has shown us that courage can be contagious, and hope can take on a life of its own.'

Keynote Address at Young African Women Leaders Forum, 22nd June 2011

★★★

Pocket Michelle Obama Wisdom

First published in 2017 by Hardie Grant Books, an imprint of
Hardie Grant Publishing

Hardie Grant Books (UK)
5th & 6th Floors
52–54 Southwark Street
London SE1 1UN
hardiegrantbooks.com

Hardie Grant Books (Australia)
Ground Floor, Building 1
658 Church Street
Melbourne, VIC 3121

British Library Cataloguing-in-Publication Data. A catalogue
record for this book is available from the British Library.

UK ISBN: 978-1-78488-131-3
US ISBN: 978-1-78488-132-0

Publisher: Kate Pollard
Senior Editor: Kajal Mistry
Editorial Assistant: Hannah Roberts
Publishing Assistant: Eila Purvis
Art Direction: Claire Warner Studio
Cover Illustration and page 32 © Kayci Wheatley, kayciwheatley.com
Cover Background © Loic Poivet. Images on pages 6 © Loic Poivet,
14 © Corpus Delicti, 54 © Karen Tyler, 69 © Chiccabubble,
88 © Bohdan Burmich, 89 © Paul Stevens, all from the Noun Project
Image on page 38 © iStock

Colour Reproduction by p2d
Printed and bound in China by Leo Paper Products Ltd.
10 9